Hello Sunshine, Goodnight Moonlight

Illustrated by

JOHN WALLACE

MACMILLAN CHILDREN'S BOOKS

To Rufus ~ J.W.

First published in 2003 by Macmillan Children's Books
A division of Macmillan Publishers Limited,
20 New Wharf Road, London N1 9RR
Basingstoke and Oxford
Associated companies throughout the world
www.panmacmillan.com

ISBN 1 405 01931 X HB
ISBN 1 405 02032 6 PB

This collection copyright © Macmillan Children's Books 2003
Illustrations copyright © John Wallace 2003

The rights of the individual poets and John Wallace to be identified as the
authors and illustrator of this work have been asserted by them in accordance
with the Copyright, Designs and Patents Act 1988.

1 3 5 7 9 8 6 4 2

A CIP catalogue record for this book is available from the British Library.

Printed in Belgium by Proost

CONTENTS

Waking Up

Oh! I have just had such a lovely dream!
And then I woke,
And all the dream went out like kettle-steam,
Or chimney-smoke.

My dream was all about – how funny, though!
I've only just
Dreamed it, and now it has begun to blow
Away like dust.

In it I went – no! in my dream I had –
No, that's not it!
I can't remember, oh, it is *too* bad,
My dream a bit.

But I saw something beautiful, I'm sure –
Then someone spoke,
And then I didn't see it any more,
Because I woke.

ELEANOR FARJEON

Cat Kisses

Sandpaper kisses
on a cheek or a chin –
that is the way
for a day to begin!

Sandpaper kisses –
a cuddle, a purr.
I have an alarm clock
that's covered with fur.

BOBBI KATZ

Toothpaste Trouble

I can use the flannel,
I can use the soap,
But when I use the toothpaste
I give up all hope.

I get
Toothpaste on my cheek,
Toothpaste on my nose,
Toothpaste on my ear,
Toothpaste on my clothes,
Toothpaste on my tummy,
Toothpaste on my knee,
And in lots of other places
That toothpaste shouldn't be!

CORAL RUMBLE

Granny, Granny, Please Comb My Hair

Granny Granny please comb
my hair
you always take your time
you always take such care

You put me on a cushion
between your knees
you rub a little coconut oil
parting gentle as a breeze

Mummy Mummy
she's always in a hurry-hurry
rush
she pulls my hair
sometimes she tugs

But Granny
you have all the time
in the world
and when you're finished
you always turn my head and say
'Now who's a nice girl?'

GRACE NICHOLS

First Day at School

A millionbillionwillion miles from home
Waiting for the bell to go. (To go where?)
Why are they all so big, other children?
So noisy? So much at home they
must have been born in uniform.
Lived all their lives in playgrounds.
Spent the years inventing games
that don't let me in. Games
that are rough, that swallow you up.

And the railings.
All around, the railings.
Are they to keep out wolves and monsters?
Things that carry off and eat children?
Things you don't take sweets from?
Perhaps they're to stop us getting out.
Running away from the lessins. Lessin.
What does a lessin look like?
Sounds small and slimy.
They keep them in glassrooms.
Whole rooms made out of glass. Imagine.

I wish I could remember my name.
Mummy said it would come in useful.
Like wellies. When there's puddles.
Yellowwellies. I wish she was here.
I think my name is sewn on somewhere.
Perhaps the teacher will read it for me.
Tea-cher. The one who makes the tea.

ROGER McGOUGH

Isn't It Amazing?

Now isn't it amazing
That seeds grow into flowers,
That grubs become bright butterflies
And rainbows come from showers,
That busy bees make honey gold
And never spend time lazing,
That eggs turn into singing birds,
Now isn't that amazing?

MAX FATCHEN

A Word

A word is dead
When it is said,
  Some say.
I say it just
Begins to live
  That day.

EMILY DICKINSON

New Sights

I like to see a thing I know
Has not been seen before,
That's why I cut my apple through
To look into the core.

It's nice to think, though many an eye
Has seen the ruddy skin,
Mine is the very first to spy
The five brown pips within.

Whiz Kid

Beth's the best at reading,
Gary's good at sums,
Kirsty's quick at counting
On her fingers and her thumbs.

Wayne's all right at writing,
Charles has lots of chums
But I'm the fastest out of school
When home time comes.

GINA DOUTHWAITE

At the End of a School Day

It is the end of a school day
  and down the long drive
come bag-swinging, shouting children.
  Deafened, the sky winces.
    The sun gapes in surprise.

Suddenly the runners skid to a stop,
  stand still and stare
at a small hedgehog
  curled up on the tarmac
    like an old, frayed cricket ball.

A girl dumps her bag, tiptoes forward
  and gingerly, so gingerly
carries the creature
  to the safety of a shady hedge.
    Then steps back, watching.

Girl, children, sky and sun
  hold their breath.
There is silence,
  a moment to remember
    on this warm afternoon in June.

WES MAGEE

Leisure

What is this life if, full of care,
We have no time to stand and stare.

No time to stand beneath the boughs
And stare as long as sheep or cows.

No time to see, when woods we pass,
Where squirrels hide their nuts in grass.

No time to see, in broad daylight,
Streams full of stars like skies at night.

No time to turn at Beauty's glance,
And watch her feet, how they can dance.

No time to wait till her mouth can
Enrich that smile her eyes began.

A poor life this if, full of care,
We have no time to stand and stare.

W.H. DAVIES

The Swing

How do you like to go up in a swing,
   Up in the air so blue?
Oh, I do think it the pleasantest thing
   Ever a child can do!

Up in the air and over the wall,
   Till I can see so wide,
Rivers and trees and cattle and all
   Over the countryside –

Till I look down on the garden green,
   Down on the roof so brown –
Up in the air I go flying again,
   Up in the air and down!

ROBERT LOUIS STEVENSON

The Vegetables Strike Back

'I don't like vegetables at all!'
Said Nathan one evening at tea.
But what the young lad didn't know
Was that vegetables hear and see.

'I don't like you as it happens,'
Said a voice from out of the mash.
'I was a fine young potato
Until you had me boiled and smashed.

'Just think how you'd like to be skinned,
Or baked alive in your jacket.
How would you feel to be crumbled up,
Then stuffed inside of a packet?

'You tear peas out of their houses
And drag them away from their mums.
You stick knives into baby beans
And forks into cucumber's bums.

'You fatten a lettuce or cabbage,
Then cut off its head with a knife.
Drive runner beans up bamboo poles
In order to choke them of life.

'I've had good friends who've been frozen,
Or left in a shed to shrink up.
Some were burned up in an oven
And some became soup in a cup.

'You spread fear round every garden
When you come to kill and destroy,
Stabbing and cutting and slicing
With your latest gardening toy.

'You say you don't like vegetables,
Well, we don't like vandals like you,
Who put us in bags and boxes,
Then drown us in steaming hot stew.'

The mouth of the boy fell open,
His fork hovered high in the air.
His knife was all ready to cut,
But now did he dare? Did he dare?

STEVE TURNER

17

A Bedtime Snack

To bed, to bed,
says Sleepy-head.
Let's bide a while, says Slow.
Put on the pot,
says Greedy-gut.
We'll sup before we go.

Hard, Hard, Hard

It's hard to lose a friend
When your heart is full of hope;
But it's worse to lose a towel
When your eyes are full of soap.

Tumbling

In jumping and tumbling
We spend the whole day,
Till night by arriving
Has finished our play.

What then? One and all,
There's no more to be said,
As we tumbled all day,
So we tumble to bed.

Bedtime

Five minutes, five minutes more please!
  Let me stay five minutes more!
Can't I just finish the castle
  I'm building here on the floor?
Can't I just finish the story
  I'm reading here in my book?
Can't I just finish this bead-chain –
  It *almost* is finished, look!
Can't I just finish this game, please?
  When a game's once begun
It's a pity never to find out
  Whether you've lost or won.
Can't I just stay five minutes?
  Well, can't I stay just four?
Three minutes, then? Two minutes?
  Can't I stay just *one* minute more?

ELEANOR FARJEON

Ten, Nine, Eight

10 small toes all washed and warm
9 soft friends in a quiet room
8 square windowpanes with falling snow
7 empty shoes in a short straight row
6 pale seashells hanging down
5 round buttons on a yellow gown
4 sleepy eyes which open and close
3 loving kisses on cheeks and nose
2 strong arms around a fuzzy bear's head
1 big girl all ready for bed

MOLLY BANG

Evensong

Evening comes on, dusk grows cold,
Bunny ears must droop and fold.
Pussy purrs, curls and sighs
Mari darling close your eyes.

All Tucked In and Roasty Toasty

All tucked in and roasty toasty
Blow me a kiss good-night
Close your eyes till morning comes
Happy dreams and sleep tight.

CLYDE WATSON

Small Things

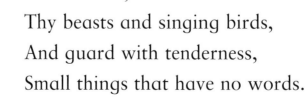

Dear Father, hear and bless
Thy beasts and singing birds,
And guard with tenderness,
Small things that have no words.

Gaelic Lullaby

Hush! the waves are rolling in,
  White with foam, white with foam;
Father toils amid the din;
  But baby sleeps at home.

Hush! the winds roar hoarse and deep,
  On they come, on they come!
Brother seeks the wandering sheep;
  But baby sleeps at home.

Hush! the rain sweeps over the knowes,
  Where they roam, where they roam;
Sister goes to seek the cows;
  But baby sleeps at home.

Bedbugs Marching Song

Bedbugs
Have the right
To bite.

Bedbugs
Of the world
Unite.

Don't let
These humans
Sleep too tight.

JOHN AGARD

Three Little Owls Who Sang Hymns

There were three little owls in a wood
Who sang hymns whenever they could;
What the words were about
One could never make out,
But one felt it was doing them good.

Young Night Thought

All night long, and every night,
When my mama puts out the light,
I see the people marching by,
As plain as day, before my eye.

Armies and emperors and kings,
All carrying different kinds of things,
And marching in so grand a way,
You never saw the like by day.

So fine a show was never seen
At the great circus on the green;
For every kind of beast and man
Is marching in that caravan.

At first they move a little slow,
But still the faster on they go,
And still beside them close I keep
Until we reach the town of Sleep.

ROBERT LOUIS STEVENSON

Crescent Moon

The crescent moon
Sails like a small boat,
Sharp at both ends.

As I sit in my small boat
I only see the shining stars
And the dark blue sky.

FROM THE TRADITIONAL CHINESE, TRANS. XIA LU

Joe Bright

By day, shut in his workshop,
Joe Bright cuts bits of tin,
And smooths them out and flattens them
Until they're paper thin.

At dusk Joe Bright flies skywards
With boxes, bags and jars,
And on the branches of the dark
He hangs a million stars.

RICHARD EDWARDS

Night

Stars over snow
   And in the west a planet
Swinging below a star –
   Look for a lovely thing and you will find it,
It is not far –
   It never will be far.

SARA TEASDALE

The Secret Song

Who saw the petals
    drop from the rose?
I, said the spider,
But nobody knows.

Who saw the sunset
    flash on a bird?
I, said the fish,
But nobody heard.

Who saw the fog
    come over the sea?
I, said the sea pigeon,
Only me.

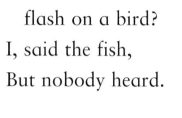

Who saw the first
    green light of the sun?
I, said the night owl,
The only one.

Who saw the moss
    creep over the stone?
I, said the gray fox,
All alone.

MARGARET WISE BROWN

New Day

The day is so new
you can hear it yawning,
listen:

The new day
is yawning
and stretching

and waiting to start.

In the clear blue sky
I hear the new day's heart.

IAN MCMILLAN

Acknowledgements

The publishers wish to thank the following for permission to use copyright material:

John Agard, 'Bedbugs Marching Song' from *We Animals Would Like a Word With You*, Bodley Head. Copyright © John Agard 1996, by permission of Caroline Sheldon Literary Agency on behalf of the author; **Molly Bang**, 'Ten, Nine, Eight' by permission of HarperCollins Inc. Copyright © 1983 Molly Bang; **W.H. Davies**, 'Leisure' from *The Complete Poems by Jonathan Cape*, by permission of the Executors of the Estate of the author; **Gina Douthwaite**, 'Whiz Kid' first published in *Countdown* by Ginn and Co., 1998. Copyright © Gina Douthwaite, by permission of the author; **Richard Edwards**, 'Joe Bright' by permission of the author. Copyright © Richard Edwards; **Eleanor Farjeon**, 'Waking Up' and 'Bedtime' from *Blackbird Has Spoken* by Macmillan Children's Books. Copyright © Eleanor Farjeon 2000, by permission of David Higham Associates on behalf of the Estate of the author; **Max Fatchen**, 'Isn't It Amazing?' from *Peculiar Rhymes and Lunatic Lines* by Max Fatchen, first published in the U.K. by Orchard Books in 1995, a division of the Watts Publishing Group Limited; **Bobbi Katz**, 'Cat Kisses'. Copyright © 1979 Bobbi Katz. Copyright © renewed 1996, by permission of the author; **Roger McGough**, 'First Day at School' from *You Tell Me*, Viking Kestrel. Reprinted by permission of PFD on behalf of Roger McGough. Copyright © Roger McGough as printed in the original volume; **Ian McMillan**, 'New Day' by permission of the author. Copyright © Ian McMillan; **Wes Magee**, 'End of the School Day' from *Matt, Wes and Pete*, by permission of the author. Copyright © Wes Magee; **Grace Nichols**, 'Granny, Granny, Please Comb My Hair' from *Come On Into My Tropical Garden*, A & C Black. Reproduced with permission of Curtis Brown Ltd, London, on behalf of Grace Nichols. Copyright © Grace Nichols, 1991; **Coral Rumble**, 'Toothpaste Trouble'. First published in *Rhymes Around the Day* by Oxford University Press. Copyright © Coral Rumble 2000, by permission of the author; **Steve Turner**, 'The Vegetables Strike Back' from *The Day I Fell Down the Toilet and Other Poems*, Lion Publishing plc. Copyright © Steve Turner 1996, by permission of the author; **Clyde Watson**, 'All Tucked In and Roasty Toasty' from *Catch Me and Kiss Me and Say It Again*, first published by William Collins Sons & Co. Copyright © Clyde Watson, 1978, by permission of Curtis Brown Ltd; **Margaret Wise Brown**; 'The Secret Song' from *Nibble, Nibble*. Text © 1959 by William R. Scott, Inc. Renewed 1987 by Roberta Brown Rauch. Used by permission of HarperCollins Publishers, New York.